A Cold Day In Hell
by

Jan Quackenbush

Published by
HaveScripts

ISBN: 9781943416264
Published by HaveScripts
Printed in the USA

A COLD DAY IN HELL

This script can be performed by community, educational, or professional theaters either for the stage, the classroom, or as reader's theater.

If you wish to perform this play, you must do the following:

1.   Purchase sufficient scripts for your performance:
•   Purchase a Multicopy PDF which allows you to print sufficient copies of this script (one for each cast member, plus 4 for the crew) at Blue Moon Plays. Click Return to Merchant to download your printable PDF. A link to the download will also be emailed to you, along with a link to the application for performance license.

OR

•   Purchase sufficient printed hard copies (one for each cast member, plus 4 for the crew) - an automatic 10 percent discount is applied to multiple printed hardcopies at the point of ordering.
2.   Apply for a performance license.
3.   Pay a Performance Fee for the specific days of your performances.

All scripts and licenses shall be obtained at Blue Moon Plays at www.havescripts.com

If you wish to make changes in the script of any kind, you must receive permission from the publisher or the playwright. Permission is usually granted readily when schools or theaters face casting problems and the changes do not affect the quality or intent of the original.

For information,
visit
www.havescripts.com
email
info@bluemoonplays.com or
call
757-816-1164

A COLD DAY IN HELL (60 minutes)
by
Jan Quackenbush

CHARLEY is behind a video camera set on a tripod; he's adjusting the focus lens to bring into clear view the spot on the sofa where he'll sit. His apartment is messy, hasn't been cleaned or tidied for a long time. He steps back, surveys the scene, then crosses to the sofa and sits, sighing like a bear.

Beside him is the camera's remote gadget which he'll use to start and stop the camera as he pleases. There's a microphone on the low coffee table before him, its cord runs back across the floor to the camera.

[There may or may not be a monitor facing the AUDIENCE showing what the camera is recording]

Once settled, he starts the camera, hunches forward, and begins, staring straight into the camera.

CHARLEY

Ok, so why am I doing this. I know that's gonna be your first question. Yeah. Why am I doing this. Right? I'll tell you. 'Cause of what they're gonna say about me. The reporters and all of them. Yeah. The cops, the lawyers, the doctors, my friends . . . maybe even you. Maybe even the government.
But what I'm saying here is this: I'm not stupid. Remember that. Charley ain't stupid. I'm not dumb. And you're gonna get it straight from the horse's mouth here. Remember that. No matter who says what about me, they don't know about it better than I know about it. So what I'm doing here is giving it to you straight off the shoulder.   I'm shooting straight off the shoulder.

1

Today it is March 16th and it is the last day for us on this earth.

(Checking his watch)

It is exactly ten seventeen . . . plus . . . twenty two seconds in the morning.

(To the camera)

Friday. End of the week. Time to check out. Yeah.   It's all over. By one o'clock this afternoon we're both gonna be dead. What I'm doing is, I'm gonna finish this up and get on over to the hospital and go into her room and disconnect the goddamn machine on her and then I'm closing shop -- I'm gonna finish myself off with the pistol I got . . . Smith and Wesson 38 caliber . . . here it is . . .

(He unbuttons his shirt in the middle and reaches inside, pulling out the pistol; holds it up for the camera)

. . . I don't know if you can see, but it's kind'a more blue than black . . . and don't worry about me having it 'cause I got a license for it . . .

(Putting it back, buttoning his shirt):

. . . no problem. And it's registered. It ain't hot.

(To the camera)

And once it's over, it's gonna put the whole damn thing to an end. And that's what you're gonna read about or see on TV. And it's gonna look like I didn't care about what I did to her. But that's stupid. That's what I call dumb. And if they wanna talk about God

2

that's Ok with me, too. But it's just as stupid as a bird without feathers. Or a rock that floats.

(He settles back a little; then)

What I'm saying here is that I care about my own damn wife more than any of those sons-a-bitches combined. And I'm doing it 'cause I love her that much to do it. Right now she's a vegetable. Yeah. She's a vegetable. She'll always be a vegetable and she can go on sprouting leaves like that as far as they're concerned until hell freezes over. And don't think they don't get paid for it, either. 'Cause they do. That's right. They get paid for keeping vegetables like her alive until they finally rot to death. But you know, and I know, that's not what she wants to be. You better believe it.

(He stares severely; then)

She's a fine lady. First and foremost. A goddamn beautiful fine lady. And she's been a terrific mother to both of you. And a terrific wife to me. Without her I'm no more than a bum. I'd be checking garbage cans. I'd be nothing. And I know her better than anybody on the face on this earth.
And what I'm doing is . . . is what I know she wants. I have no doubt. No fear. I ain't flinching. And what I'm doing to myself is what I know I want. So . . .

So just make damn sure you put us both in the ground together. Side by side. For that perpetual eternity you hear about. That's all I'm asking. No buts. I don't wanna hear no arguments about that. Get us out there to that Overview Cemetery off'a Ocean Drive where I got the plots and drop us down there and go home. Period. (Pauses; then): Ok. I'm gonna take a little break here. So time out. But don't go no where 'cause I ain't done yet. Hang on.

(He stops the camera with his remote gadget.
Drinks from a glass of water that's beside the microphone- -
gargles- - then swallows. Stares. Then starts the camera):

You gotta understand I'm not pretending to be no hero. Acting like I was God or anything like that. If they say that crap about me, I'm telling it to you different. If I was a hero, say, I'd be giving my organs to medicine. And if I was a God I'd have cured her 6 months ago. Hell. If I was a God she wouldn't a had the accident in the first place! (Pauses; then): Forget it. God don't exist for me. Used to, though. You know that. How many times we ever miss church on Sundays? That's right. Almost never. Think about it. Go ahead. You want some time?. . . I'll give you time . . . (long pause; then): Right. Almost never. And we always put our money in the plate, too. Sometimes I felt like I was dead broke, but I dished it out anyway. And if I'm wrong, if God's really up there, and we get to meet -- which doesn't seem too likely under the circumstances -- it's gonna be pretty damn interesting to hear Him answering a coupla questions I got. Starting with how come He lets beautiful and wonderful people like your mother suffer and die without a reason that'd make sense to even a monkey, while all the bums and murderers and rapists and flakey dictators can keep on getting their jollies off? For what reason? For what kind'a holy reason does He let the good people suffer and the bad ones keep having picnics? And don't go telling me it's to teach us by experience like Father Hildebrant says, either. That's a lot of crap. What it is, is a conspiracy ... to keep us on our knees with our heads down and mumbling prayers so that someone can come up and kick us over and get away with it. But not me.

I'm not falling for it no more. Un-unnh. Your old man's had it up to here. Hell, I've been on my knees praying for her ever since it happened and not a goddamn thing has changed! Nothing! Nothings changed! And it won't. . . not until I go in there and

4

change it myself. Yeah. And I'll tell you somethinq else . . . I'm following a Commandment. "Do unto others as you'd have'em do to you."

That's right. 'Cause if I was in her shoes I'd want her to do the same thing to me. Un-plug. Let me go. Whoosh. Just like that. Right into heaven. Only difference being I wouldn't want her hurting herself afterwards. No.
But . . . that'd be her choice. I'm choosing my own choice. There's no point in me living without her. Hell. You don't need me. This apartment don't need me . . . city don't need me, country don't need me . . . goddamn WORLD don't need me . . . the dog don't need me.

Ok, break, break. Time out. This is tough. I gotta . . .

>   *(He's lowering his head to his chest, waving his*
>   *hands in the air at the camera; finally reaches*
>   *for the gadget and stops it. Then; to himself):*

Yeah. Real tough. Calm down, Charlie. Ya gotta calm down. Or you ain't gonna make it. Someone'll stop you in the parking lot for being so edgy.

(He stands after a moment, crosses to the camera, and stares through it to the sofa. Then he moves and crosses back to pick up the microphone and remote gadget, and speaks while standing, staring into camera lense):

Can you see me? Yeah. New angle. New way of seeing an old thing. *(Slight, strained grin; then):* Look. Mercy killing. When it's being talked about . . . like on TV . . . what they do is, they talk about morality. But I remember when Joe Pirello was running for sidewalk commissioner he wanted to give me five bucks to vote for him. Did I ever tell this story? I told him, "Hey, Joe, come on. You know you got my vote. We grew up together for chrissakes!" "Hey," he says. "I'm just offering to defray your gas to get to the poll to vote." So he gets elected, and then what happens? He widens the sidewalk out here which takes out a chunk of the yard where your mother had flowers growing. Fifteen years she had flowers growing there. Remember all her tulips and zinnias? Hunh?

(Stares severely; then)

And how'd I lose my job? Talk about moralitv. Blow it out your ears. Eighteen years plus . . . I'm one of the best goddamn machinist around. You know that. Hey, how many calls I get in the middle of the night to go down there and fix something some screwball gummed up? So what'd they do?

Up-graded the boss's nephew outta college and knocked me out. A kid so dumb he couldn't even open the snap on his lunchbox. And even my union., after all the dues I paid in year after year, it didn't lift a finger for me. Yeah. So here's to the union. (He gives it the finger.) But they got theirs. You bet they did. All of'em. 'Cause now you can walk around the shop and hear a pin drop 'cause they moved the whole operation to Korea. Which is the biggest laugh in the world 'cause I fought over there. So what kind of "morality" is that? Hunh? Think about it. And now they wanna spend it all in South America in the Amazon propping up even more dictators. Yeah. Or else on sand dunes.

Or more missiles when we already got enough to sink the, be-jesus out of all the countries combined right down to the bottom of the ocean. And then . . . then you read about what they're gonna say about ME for taking away the suffering of one of the most beautiful human beings that ever walked this planet. I'll tell you something. I know I taught you kids to grow up respecting your parents and the laws. ... right? ... to grow up respecting what keeps everybody normal and not an animal . . . but if I had to do it all over again, I'd tell you to go live in the woods and make a little room for me and your mother, too. We'd go on up into Maine, or else Oregon, maybe Alaska, and eat moose meat.

I mean it. Some of the crap they spread in this country would kill a field of garlic. That's just the way I feel about it. And here I am saying this, your father, who pulled his handkerchief out at the Lincoln Memorial that time we was all visiting Washington, D.C.. (Pauses; then): See . . . I got a new angle on things, too.

(Pauses; then): Break. (He stops the camera.)

(He re-aims the camera angle to his spot on the sofa; crosses to the sofa, and sits. Starts the camera, sets the gadget on the table)

Look. I don't wanna sound like I'm making a big deal out of a small pan of fish. You know me better than that, for chrissakes. And you're looking at me sitting here like I'm calm as a cucumber. But inside . . . right here . . . it's like an earthquake cracking my ribs apart. I'm feeling like Mount St. Helen inside.

You get to a point where there's nothing you can do about nothing. You can't save your wife from dying- - or from being dead but living. I'm just telling you the facts of my developing the course of action I told you about. But what I'm saying here is something else, too. I'm saying that even though the world generally stinks, once in a while you get a sunny day. And you have to appreciate that. That's a home run. My best sunny day was when Betty said she'd marry me. And she was crying she was so happy I asked her.

And another sunny day for us would'a been when you were born, Bill. And then you, Marge. You were another sunny day. We were just goddamn lucky to pull you two wonderful kids out of the hat like we did. And who got through school without being dope addicts. Or pregnant. Or stabbed in the cafeteria for not handing over a peanut butter sandwich like what's his name got it. I'll tell you something. You're more than home runs. You kids and your mother are the whole damn ball game. Ok, so . . .

What I wanna tell you, that whole thing about sunny days and so on, is that just because I'm closing shop it doesn't mean you're suppose to go out and do something crazy when things get tough. Are you listening!?

I don't want you following in my footsteps. I mean it.
Just keep your nose to the grindstone and count your blessings.

You got some beautiful kids there, both of you. It's been fun for us to be grandparents. And, Bill, you got yourself a terrific wife there, too. She keeps you cleaned up and walking straight. I know that. You don't go down to the racetrack and throw away your money on a bunch of mules like you used to do. I'm proud of you, believe me. And so isn't Betty. She used to brag about you even in the supermarket. That goes for you, too, Marge. Your kids are the spittin' image. And even though I sometimes think your husband's off the wall a little, I'm not so blind I can't see he loves you more than anything. So that is two pluses for both of you. What I'm doing I'm not saying is for you to do or anybody else to do. There's too much of that copy-cat stuff, and it's ruining the country. All you gotta do is read the paper to see how every Tom, Dick, and Harry is taking the law into his own hands whenever he's pissed off about something. That's not what I'm doing. I'm not doing it because I'm pissed off. I want that understood. I'm doing it because I love your mother more than anything else in the world,

8

and I'm not gonna stay home here and eat a sandwich and drink a beer while she's . . . artificial.

There's enough of that in this world to sink a navy. Ok. So when you get a problem don't go and do anything crazy. When you get old like your folks, if you get hit with a tragedy that's a major, then you make your own decisions, but up until then you give things time to work themselves out. Am I making sense? I think I am making sense because primarily you got yourselves some beautiful kids who are counting on you. As far as Betty and I go, you kids are grown up and you don't need us anymore to lead you around. I'm not exactly an encyclopedia of knowledge and rare and useful facts you're not gonna get from anvbody else.

> (*He stares into the camera, hopelessly lost,*
> *slipping nearer to self-pity*)

What we u'sta say in the shop is that something's what you call "obsolete."

(*He pauses, uncertain where this line of thought   is leading,*
fearful of self-betrayal; but, then, pushes on)

Even a grandfather's obsolete anymore 'cause the kids all got television and what-cha call "video" games, and they wanna visit about as much as they wanna enema.

> (*He frowns; then*)

I'll tell you something else. If you kids were here visiting with me I wouldn't have to be talking into this camera-- that doesn't know me from Adam. And I wouldn't have spent the money to rent it, either. But, hey, don't get me wrong 'cause I'm not sayinq I'm angry about it. I can't go asking Bill to take time off and spend the

9

money to get out here from California just because I'm closing shop, and that goes for you, too, Marge. Wisconsin's far enough away it might as well be Antartica. And, besides, you guys were out here 6 months ago anyway, right after the accident, and I appreciate that, like I told you. Plus, like I said, I don't go around expecting miracles.

> *(Stares into the camera; then more to the point,*
> *less whiny, his thoughts clearer)*

Even if you was here, I got my doubts you'd be able to stop me from going ahead with this. You'd hafta come up with a pretty goddamn good reason or else knock me out.

About the only way I can see myself stalling on this would be if I was to take off and visit you guys. But then that would be shafting Betty who even though she doesn't know it when I'm sitting next to her by the bed there, you don't know that she's not hearing anything when Im talking to her. *(Pauses; then)* Time out. I'm getting a leg cramp or something.

> *(He stands . . . kicking his right leg out a*
> *couple times . . . approaches AUDIENCE - the*
> *camera - massages his cramped leg; as)*

I was just . . . going through my mind . . . how I can
. . . sit next to Betty there and talk about the weather or a ballgame or the leak in the roof- - nothing serious, just another goddamn annoyance when I least need it- - but I'm sitting there making small talk, and . . . I didn't use to, you-know. I used to talk about reasons for living, stuff like that. I'd say, like, "Betty, what you are going through is like a hibernation, so do not worry about it 'cause your body knows what it is doing, and what it is doing is fixing itself up from the inside and keeping you asleep . . .

(patting his leg hard): . . . so you do not stir things up!"

(He brings his hands up helplessly, and shrugs; then)

I do not talk to her about her brain. I do not talk to her about that 'cause that is the center of her problem as far as I can understand from what the doctors tell me. You'd need a dictionary to understand them half the time. But, anyway, there is this thing about one side of her brain taking over the workload of the other side- - they told me to think of it like changing shifts in a factory - - but what I am saying is if I was talking to her about her brain I don't know what side I'm talking to, and if she is hearing me I don't wanna go and screw things up in there.

> *(He stares a brief moment- - apologetic,*
> *baffled; then)*

Hey, maybe you think that's stupid, but there's a lot of things that look stupid in this world which, believe me, if you knew more about it they might be smart. And I don't pretend to be a genius like there's a lot of phonies that do!

> *(Squirms, relaxes a little, then)*

So . . . what I do not do is I do not talk to her about her brain. And for a while there, I was talking to her about what sounded to me like some pretty good reasons for living. *(Pauses; then):* Usually, though, I'd end up with me as being the main reason.

> *(Pauses., then)*

Maybe you think that's a joke, but I was trying to give her something to hang her hat on.

*(He stares, then drinks water from the glass;
then)*

So . . . I would start out by giving her little things- - sort of like I am dishing out photographs- - "I am not any good in our apartment," I'd say, "by myself. Things are not getting put away." Stuff like that. Stuff she could probably see without thinking about. How I am only eating from a can, or a frozen dinner, since I cannot even boil water- - which she knows is not true, but is close enough she is not gonna argue. Once I even took in a list of things to read to her so she'd get a sense of how things are really falling apart. I only did that once, though, 'cause I could see it could backfire on me. She might just decide that was it. So then I took in some actual photographs of hers and remembered them to her. That seemed like it was Ok. Besides, you know, some of them are good.

I was the main reason, though, I could think of for her to get better and back on her feet. Sometimes I would just hint about it, and other times I'd come right out and say it. "Betty, a lot of people love you and are rooting for you - I have letters that would make you cry - and I could make up a list a mile long if I had to, but nobody loves you like I do and I swear to God that if you need one main reason to get through this, and get well, and go through all the recuperations and therapies, and put up with the nurses and the doctors and the medicine, then I'm telling you to do it for me because without you coming back to me it would take a cold day in hell for me to wanna live myself or even see another sunny day." Period.

But I said that lately I got into small talk, remember? I stopped giving her reasons for living on my account because something started to gnaw at me from the inside like a rat. I'm a nobody. I've been good to her, and decent and honest as a husband and as a father, and faithful to her- - hey, not that I've never looked at

12

another pair of legs, I'll admit it, but that's not a big deal once you cut the cards, not a crime like what you think of as a crime- - but then you add up the rest of me and, OK, I'm clean but I'm a nobody, too. I'm Charley, and that's it. I don't know when it hit me like that- - maybe it was when I was telling her why she ought to pull through and I couldn't tell if I was making an impact or not. An impression. She never flinched or gave me a sign. Or maybe I'd just gotten home from a visit with her and was putting the key in the lock when it dawned on me that this is all I am-- somebody with a crummy apartment and no job and a family that's broken all to hell like a plastic toy. So, I can't go in there anymore and pretend I've got a pair of aces up my sleeve that's gonna make her life any better than the goddamn hard work it was before. So the next day is when I started just telling her about the weather and the ballgames and the leak in the roof - which I made into a real story so I could add to it a little bit each day. Not that I ever thought I was a big-shot in the first place. You know that. When did you ever hear me say I was a big-shot? Never. And she knows that. And she loved me for what I am anyway. But you'd have to be a jerk to think it's worth it for her to go through what she's going through for me. What you have to do . . .

(He seems suddenly inspired by these thoughts)

. . . what you have to do in a case like this is put the shoe on the other foot. If I had'a come back to me, I'd wanna close DOWN!

(He falls back: morose)

Besides. . . all this talk about pulling through is a foul ball. Malarky. What the doctors say is her chances just to wake up, just to wake up, for chrissakes . . . that's one in a million. It could happen, but, like somebody told me, the moon would probably hit the earth first. (Pauses; then): And even if she did, what's in it for her? You gotta ask yourself that question. Bill? Marge? What the hell is in it for her anyway?

(Suddenly jumping to his feet)

I can't keep sittin'! And I don't feel good.

(Pauses; then)

Ok, I'm gonna ask you something. If what God does is a mystery, then how come when you put all the people
together who ever lived you can't solve it? *(Pauses; then)*: You got an answer for that? How come you can't
solve it? We can send people to the moon. Build cars. Television sets. This camera that's staring at me like
nut. But if you put all our brains together like jellyfish in row on a beach and wrap it around the world a few times you still couldn't make a damn bit of sense out of what God does. How come? How come your mother has to have a car accident on a sunny day on her way to the goddamn laundromat and end up in a coma for chrissakes when you can't even count the number of people she's ever hurt 'cause there aren't any!?

(He stares severely; then)

That's no mystery. . . it's a crime. A real crime. What I'm gonna do is a picnic compared to that. And if you're telling me that somehow it's for her own good, you're crazier than a dog that's got rabies. You'll never make any sense out of this'one, buddy. And if you try, they might as well lock you up and throw away the key.

(Starts pacing)

14

Jesus Christ! This world's the pits! The living pits! And she's just one out of, Christ, I can't tell you how many people that are in the same boat. And why? For what reason? Tell me!

(Pauses - staring, clearly baffled - anger rising)

And . . . why the hell . . . why the hell are all those people who never did anythinq to anybody qetting shot in the ass all over South America? Or over there in the mid-east? Even Ireland, for chrissakes - which used to be run by the monks! Remember? And Kosovo. You get this stuff on the news every night of the week!

(Pacing)

So why the hell does God let some piss-ant whacko dictator live for when he's got beautiful and decent people like Betty who goes to church her whole damn life and prays to Him and puts money in the plate and drinks His blood . . . and how does she end up? . . . how does she spell relief? suffering as much as the people she prayed to Him to help out?

And I'm telling you the list is beyond belief! You oughta see the ward she's on. They need computers just to keep track of them. All over the city. All over the city there's these dead people kept alive. In our own country, for chrissakes! America! Hey! Big dream! Big melting pot! From shore to shining shore. Hell, you put all the Betty's together and you'd get one HELL OF A BIG DREAM!! About no more SUFFERING! JESUS CHRIST! TAKE ME AWAY! I can't understand it. I just can't. All I can do is BEAT MY HEAD AGAINST THE WALL!

I can't look at anybody anymore without seeing them as a victim . . . yeah .. . as a victim of . . . something.

Aagh! Forget it. Just forget it. Try to think positive.

(Looks away, frowning. Then back)

Yeah, "positive." Look . . . if I had more time, I'd get out there and do something to help. You better believe it. I've had it up to here with people that just sit around whineing . . . crying like babies about their problems and not doing anything about it. And I'm not talking politics, either. Politics is broken promises as far as I'm concerned. There's some that aren't bad. And all you can do is beat your head against the wall and hope they stay clean. But what I'm talking about is "assistance." Getting involved inna organization--that isn't full of weirdos --to help people who are caving under. Not just poor people, either. I don't give a damn if you're rich or poor -- I've never met a poor person who was better than a rich person just because he is poor. If you're caving under you're caving under. I could pick from alot of organizations to get involved. Take your Red Cross, for example. Or March of Dimes. Or maybe something smaller . . . something in the neighborhood . . . like the Boy Scouts. Yeah. I'll bet I could help'em grow up to be good citizens . . . round off some of the rough edges in the world . . . reduce the crime rate.

(Pauses; then)

I'll   give you a statistic for you: Most of the crimes committed in America are committed by people who are caving under. Did you know that?

(He stares severely; then)

'Cause you need help.

(He nods; then)

Ok, I wanna bring this to a close, and let you go. As far as my last will and testiment goes, it's in my safety deposit box over at Somona Savings bank. I won't go into it here, but it's not much. And as far as the law goes, I'm not sure what's gonna happen to my insurance policy . . . on account of beneficiaries not collecting from suicides. But you're both set pretty well anyhow. So. . . so much for that. What else is there to say except I'll tell you one more time that I love you both more than anything in the world. And keep your chin up no matter what. And forget what anybody's gonna say about me because it's probably not gonna be nice. It's not even gonna be the truth. But it's gonna be for real . . . 'cause now I have the guts to stand up for what I believe, and follow through on this. Your dad's a strong man.

Ok . . . so I just want you to know one more thing. Two more things. The first is this: Betty's accident. I didn't tell you this before. When you were right here afterwards. But . . . it was meant for me. Or else, I mean, it might not have happened. And that is . . . because . . . Betty had asked me to take the clothes down to the laundromat. She was not feeling good. I said no.

(Pauses; then)

I don't like to hang around there. The only guys there are bums. Or guys like me . . . without work. I see them, they see me. You know what I mean? I just don't like to hang around there. So she went, and not feeling good. She wasn't mad at me. She knows I don't like that place. She only asked me because she was . . . sick.

(Stares; then)

Then I get the phone call. *(Pauses)* So, you see, it didn't have to happen did it. But it did. And the only thing I can do is close shop.

17

(He drinks water, his hand shaking; then)

The second thing is this: this is not the first time I have done this .
. . gone out, I mean, and rented this camera to explain what I am
going to do. This is my third time. The first time, it was too
complicated. I could not get it to work right. The second time,
which was the last time . . . I do not think I said things right. I left
some of it out, too. But now I think I said things right, and it is all
there. I am feeling a little cold about it, but it is all there just the
same. And who knows? Maybe feeling cold about it makes it
easier. Each time I seem to feel colder.

I just hope to God. . . that when I see Betty today . . I'm cold like
ice. That I don't melt. I'm all frozen stiff inside sub-zero. . . or else
. . . God help me. . . that if I should sit down beside her, rub her
cheek, brush her hair back, I could . . . I could <u>thaw</u> . . . just
enough. . .just enough to decide to give it one more day.

(He stares at the camera a moment, then stops it.
He crosses to EXIT as)

LIGHTS fade to Blackout

THE END

A COLD DAY IN HELL (30 minutes)
By
Jan Quackenbush

CHARLEY is behind a video camera set on a tripod; he's adjusting the focus lens to bring into clear view the spot on the sofa where he'll sit. His apartment is messy, hasn't been cleaned or tidied for a long time. He steps back, surveys the scene, then crosses to the sofa and sits, sighing like a bear.

Beside him is the camera's remote gadget which he'll use to start and stop the camera as he pleases. There's a microphone on the low coffee table before him, its cord runs back across the floor to the camera.

> *[There may or may not be a monitor facing the AUDIENCE showing what the camera is recording]*

Once settled, he starts the camera, hunches forward, and begins, staring straight into the camera.

CHARLEY:
Ok, so why am I doing this. I know that's gonna be your first question. Yeah. Why am I doing this. Right? I'll tell you. 'Cause of what they're gonna say about me. The reporters and all of them. Yeah. The cops, the lawyers, the doctors, my friends . . . maybe even you. Maybe even the government.

But what I'm saying here is this: I'm not stupid. Remember that. Charley ain't stupid. I'm not dumb. And you're gonna get it straight from the horse's mouth here. Remember that. No matter who says what about me, they don't know about it better than I know about it. So what I'm doing here is giving it to you straight

off the shoulder.   I'm shooting straight off the shoulder.
Today it is March 16th and it is the last day for us on this earth.

(Checking his watch)

It is exactly ten seventeen . . . plus . . . twenty two seconds in the
morning.

(To the camera)

Friday. End of the week. Time to check out. Yeah.   It's all over. By
one o'clock this afternoon we're both gonna be dead. What I'm
doing is, I'm gonna finish this up and get on over to the hospital
and go into her room and disconnect the goddamn machine on
her and then I'm closing shop -- I'm gonna finish myself off with
the pistol I got . . . Smith and Wesson 38 caliber . . . here it is . . .

*(He unbuttons his shirt in the middle and reaches inside, pulling
out the pistol; holds it up for the camera)*

. . . I don't know if you can see, but it's kind'a more blue than
black . . . and don't worry about me having it 'cause I got a license
for it . . .

(Putting it back, buttoning his shirt):

. . . no problem. And it's registered. It ain't hot.

(To the camera):

And once it's over, it's gonna put the whole damn thing to an end.
And that's what you're gonna read about or see on TV. And it's
gonna look like I didn't care about what I did to her. But that's
stupid. That's what I call dumb. And if they wanna talk about God
that's Ok with me, too. But it's just as stupid as a bird without
feathers. Or a rock that floats.

(He settles back a little; then):

What I'm saying here is that I care about my own damn wife more
than any of those sons-a-bitches combined. And I'm doing it
'cause I love her that much to do it. Right now she's a vegetable.
Yeah. She's a vegetable. She'll always be a vegetable and she can
go on sprouting leaves like that as far as they're concerned until

hell freezes over. And don't think they don't get paid for it, either. 'Cause they do. That's right. They get paid for keeping vegetables like her alive

until they finally rot to death. But you know, and I know, that's not what she wants to be. You better believe it.

(He stares severely; then):

She's a fine lady. First and foremost. A goddamn beautiful fine lady. And she's been a terrific mother to both of you. And a terrific wife to me. Without her I'm no more than a bum. I'd be checking garbage cans. I'd be nothing. And I know her better than anybody on the face on this earth.

And what I'm doing is . . . is what I know she wants. I have no doubt. No fear. I ain't flinching. And what I'm doing to myself is what I know I want. So . . .

So just make damn sure you put us both in the ground together. Side by side. For that perpetual eternity you hear about. That's all I'm asking. No buts. I don't wanna hear no arguments about that. Get us out there to that Overview Cemetery off'a Ocean Drive where I got the plots and drop us down there and go home. Period. (Pauses; then): Ok. I'm gonna take a little break here. So time out. But don't go no where 'cause I ain't done yet. Hang on.

(He stops the camera with his remote gadget.
Drinks from a glass of water that's beside the microphone-
- gargles- - then swallows. Stares. Then starts the camera):

You gotta understand I'm not pretending to be no hero. Acting like I was God or anything like that. If they say that crap about me, I'm telling it to you different. If I was a hero, say, I'd be giving my organs to medicine. And if I was a God I'd have cured her 6 months ago. Hell. If I was a God she wouldn't a had the accident in the first place! (Pauses; then): Forget it. God don't exist for me. Used to, though. You know that. How many times we ever miss

church on Sundays? That's right. Almost never. Think about it. Go
ahead. You want some time?. . . I'll give you time . . . (long pause;
then): Right. Almost never. And we always put our money in the
plate, too. Sometimes I felt like I was dead broke, but I dished it
out anyway. And if I'm wrong, if God's really up there, and we get
to meet -- which doesn't seem too likely under the circumstances
-- it's gonna be pretty damn interesting to hear Him answering a
coupla questions I got. Starting with how come He lets beautiful
and wonderful people like your mother suffer and die without a
reason that'd make sense to even a monkey, while all the bums
and murderers and rapists and flakey dictators can keep on
getting their jollies off? For what reason? And don't go telling me
it's to teach us by experience like Father Hildebrant says, either.
That's a lot of crap. What it is, is a conspiracy ... to keep us on our
knees with our heads down and mumbling prayers so that
someone can come up and kick us over and get away with it. But
not me.

I'm not falling for it no more.

Hell, I've been on my knees praying for her ever since it happened
and not a goddamn thing has changed! Nothing! And I'll tell you
somethinq else . . . I'm following a Commandment. "Do unto
others as you'd have'em do to you."
That's right. 'Cause if I was in her shoes I'd want her to do the
same thing to me. Un-plug. Let me go. Whoosh. Just like that.
Right into heaven. Only difference being I wouldn't want her
hurting herself afterwards. No.
But . . . that'd be her choice. I'm choosing my own choice.
There's no point in me living without her. Hell. You don't need me.
This apartment don't need me . . . city don't need me, country
don't need me . . . goddamn WORLD don't need me . . . the dog
don't need me.

22

Ok, break, break. Time out. This is tough. I gotta . . .

(He's lowering his head to his chest, waving his
hands in the air at the camera; finally reaches
for the gadget and stops it. Then; to himself):

Yeah. Real tough. Calm down, Charlie. Ya gotta calm down. Or you
ain't gonna make it. Someone'll stop you in the parking lot for
being so edgy.

(He stands after a moment, crosses to the camera, and
stares through it to the sofa. Then he moves and crosses
back to pick up the microphone and remote gadget, and
speaks while standing, staring into camera lense):

Can you see me? Yeah. New angle. New way of seeing an old
thing. (Slight, strained grin; then): Look. Mercy killing. When it's
being talked about . . . like on TV . . . what they do is, they talk
about morality. But I remember when Joe Pirello was running for
sidewalk commissioner he wanted to give me five bucks to vote
for him. Did I ever tell this story? I told him, "Hey, Joe, come on.
You know you got my vote. We grew up together for chrissakes!"
"Hey," he says. "I'm just offering to defray your gas to get to the
poll to vote." So he gets elected, and then what happens? He
widens the sidewalk out here which takes out a chunk of the yard
where your mother had flowers growing. Fifteen years she had
flowers growing there. Remember all her tulips and zinnias?
Hunh?

(Stares severely; then):

And how'd I lose my job? Talk about morality. Blow it out your
ears. Eighteen years plus . . . I'm one of the best goddamn
machinist around. You know that. Hey, how many calls I get in the

middle of the night to go down there and fix something some screwball gummed up? So what'd they do?

Up-graded the boss's nephew outta college and knocked me out. A kid so dumb he couldn't even open the snap on his lunchbox. And even my union., after all the dues I paid in year after year, it didn't lift a finger for me. Yeah. So here's to the union. (He gives it the finger.) But they got theirs. You bet they did. All of'em. 'Cause now you can walk around the shop and hear a pin drop'cause they moved the whole operation to Korea. Which is the biggest laugh in the world 'cause I fought over there. So what kind of "morality" is that? Hunh? Think about it. And now they wanna spend it all in South America in the Amazon propping up even more dictators. Yeah. Or else on sand dunes.

And then . . . then you read about what they're gonna say about ME for taking away the suffering of one of the most beautiful human beings that ever walked this planet. I'll tell you something. I know I taught you kids to grow up respecting your parents and the laws. ... right? ... to grow up respecting what keeps everybody normal and not an animal . . . but if I had to do it all over again, I'd tell you to go live in the woods and make a little room for me and your mother, too. We'd go on up into Maine, or else Oregon, maybe Alaska, and eat moose meat.

(Pauses; then): See . . . I got a new angle on things, too.

(Pauses; then): Break. (He stops the camera.)

> (He re-aims the camera angle to his spot on the sofa; crosses to the sofa, and sits. Starts the camera, sets the gadget on the table):

Look. I don't wanna sound like I'm making a big deal out of a small pan of fish. You know me better than that, for chrissakes. And you're looking at me sitting here like I'm calm as a cucumber. But inside . . . right here . . . it's like an earthquake cracking my ribs apart. I'm feeling like Mount St. Helen inside.

You get to a point where there's nothing you can do about nothing. You can't save your wife from dying- - or from being dead but living. I'm just telling you the facts of my developing the course of action I told you about. But what I'm saying here is something else, too. I'm saying that even though the world generally stinks, once in a while you get a sunny day. And you have to appreciate that. That's a home run. My best sunny day was when Betty said she'd marry me. And she was crying she was so happy I asked her.
And another sunny day for us would'a been when you were born, Bill. And then you, Marge. You were another sunny day. We were just goddamn lucky to pull you two wonderful kids out of the hat like we did. And who got through school without being dope addicts. Or pregnant. Or stabbed in the cafeteria for not handing over a peanut butter sandwich like what's his name got it. I'll tell you something. You're more than home runs. You kids and your mother are the whole damn ball game. Ok, so . . .

What I wanna tell you, that whole thing about sunny days and so on, is that just because I'm closing shop it doesn't mean you're suppose to go out and do something crazy when things get tough. Are you listening!?

I don't want you following in my footsteps. I mean it.
Just keep your nose to the grindstone and count your blessings. You got some beautiful kids there, both of you. It's been fun for us to be grandparents. And, Bill, you got yourself a terrific wife there, too. She keeps you cleaned up and walking straight. I know that. You don't go down to the racetrack and throw away your money

on a bunch of mules like you used to do. I'm proud of you, believe me. And Betty. She used to brag about you even in the supermarket. That goes for you, too, Marge. Your kids are the spittin' image. And even though I sometimes think your husband's off the wall a little, I'm not so blind I can't see he loves you more than anything. So that is two pluses for both of you. What I'm doing I'm not saying is for you to do or anybody else to do. There's too much of that copy-cat stuff, and it's ruining the country. All you gotta do is read the paper to see how every Tom, Dick, and Harry is taking the law into his own hands whenever he's pissed off about something. That's not what I'm doing. I'm not doing it because I'm pissed off. I want that understood. I'm doing it because I love your mother more than anything else in the world, and I'm not gonna stay home here and eat a sandwich and drink a beer while she's . . . artificial.

There's enough of that in this world to sink a navy. Ok. So when you get a problem don't go and do anything crazy. When you get old like your folks, if you get hit with a tragedy that's a major, then you make your own decisions, but up until then you give things time to work themselves out. Am I making sense? I think I am making sense because primarily you got yourselves some beautiful kids who are counting on you. As far as Betty and I go, you kids are grown up and you don't need us anymore to lead you around

> (He stares into the camera, hopelessly lost,
> slipping nearer to self-pity):

What we u'sta say in the shop is that something's what you call "obsolete."

I'll tell you something else. If you kids were here visiting with me I wouldn't have to be talking into this camera—that doesn't know

26

me from Adam. And I wouldn't have spent the money to rent it, either. But, hey, don't get me wrong 'cause I'm not sayinq I'm angry about it. I can't go asking Bill to take time off and spend the money to get out here from California just because I'm closing shop, and that goes for you, too, Marge. Wisconsin's far enough away it might as well be Antartica. And, besides, you guys were out here 6 months ago anyway, right after the accident, and I appreciate that, like I told you. Plus, like I said, I don't go around expecting miracles.

(Stares into the camera; then more to the point, less whiny, his thoughts clearer):

Even if you was here, I got my doubts you'd be able to stop me from going ahead with this. You'd hafta come up with a pretty goddamn good reason or else knock me out.

(He stands . . . kicking his right leg out a couple times . . . approaches AUDIENCE - the camera - massages his cramped leg; as):

I was just . . . going through my mind . . . how I can . . . sit next to Betty there and talk about the weather or a ballgame or the leak in the roof- - nothing serious, just another goddamn annoyance when I least need it- - but I'm sitting there making small talk, and . . . I didn't use to, you-know. I used to talk about reasons for living, stuff like that. I'd say, like, "Betty, what you are going through is like a hibernation, so do not worry about it 'cause your body knows what it is doing, and what it is doing is fixing itself up from the inside and keeping you asleep . . . (patting his leg hard): . . . so you do not stir things up!"

(He brings his hands up helplessly, and shrugs; then):

27

I do not talk to her about her brain. I do not talk to her about that 'cause that is the center of her problem as far as I can understand from what the doctors tell me. You'd need a dictionary to understand them half the time. But, anyway, there is this thing about one side of her brain taking over the workload of the other side- - they told me to think of it like changing shifts in a factory - - but what I am saying is if I was talking to her about her brain I don't know what side I'm talking to, and if she is hearing me I don't wanna go and screw things up in there.

>(He stares a brief moment- - apologetic.,
>baffled; then):

Hey, maybe you think that's stupid, but there's alot of things that look stupid in this world which, believe me, if you knew more about it they might be smart. And I don't pretend to be a genius like there's alot of phonies that do!

>(Squirms, relaxes a little, then):

So . . . what I do not do is I do not talk to her about her brain. And for a while there, I was talking to her about what sounded to me like some pretty good reasons for living. (Pauses; then): Usually, though, I'd end up with me as being the main reason.
>(Pauses., then):

Maybe you think that's a joke, but I was trying to give her something to hang her hat on.

>(He stares, then drinks water from the glass;
>then):

So . . . I would start out by giving her little things- - sort of like I am dishing out photographs- - "I am not any good in our apartment,"

28

I'd say, "by myself. Things are not getting put away." Stuff like that. Stuff she could probably see without thinking about. How I am only eating from a can, or a frozen dinner, since I cannot even boil water- - which she knows is not true, but is close enough she is not gonna argue. Once I even took in a list of things to read to her so she'd get a sense of how things are really falling apart. I only did that once, though, 'cause I could see it could backfire on me. She might just decide that if things are falling apart why bother to live anymore? So then I took in some actual photographs of hers and remembered them to her. That seemed like it was Ok. Besides, you know, some of them are good.

I was the main reason, though, I could think of for her to get better and back on her feet. Sometimes I would just hint about it, and other times I'd come right out and say it. "Betty, a lot of people love you and are rooting for you - I have letters that would make you cry - and I could make up a list a mile long if I had to, but nobody loves you like I do and I swear to God that if you need one main reason to get through this, and get well, and go through all the recuperations and therapies, and put up with the nurses and the doctors and the medicine, then I'm telling you to do it for me because without you coming back to me it would take a cold day in hell for me to wanna live myself or even see another sunny day." Period.

But I said that lately I got into small talk, remember? I stopped giving her reasons for living on my account because something started to gnaw at me from the inside like a rat. I'm a nobody. I've been good to her, and decent and honest as a husband and as a father, and faithful to her- - hey, not that I've never looked at another pair of legs, I'll admit it, but that's not a big deal once you cut the cards, not a crime like what you think of as a crime- - but then you add up the rest of me and, OK, I'm clean but I'm a nobody, too. I'm Charley, and that's it. But when I was telling her why she ought to pull through, I couldn't tell if I was making an impact or not. An impression. She never flinched or gave me a sign. One day, I started just telling her about the weather and the ballgames and the leak in the roof - which I made into a real story so I could add to it a little bit each day. Not that I ever thought I was a big-shot in the first place. You know that. When did you ever hear me say I was a big-shot? Never. And she knows that. And she loved me for what I am anyway. But you'd have to be a jerk to think it's worth it for her to go through what she's going through for me. What you have to do . . .

(He seems suddenly inspired by these thoughts):

. . . what you have to do in a case like this is put the shoe on the other foot. If I had'a come back to me, I'd wanna close DOWN!

(He falls back: morose):

Besides. . . all this talk about pulling through is a foul ball. Malarky. What the doctors say is her chances just to wake up, just to wake up, for chrissakes . . . that's one in a million. It could happen, but, like somebody told me, the moon would probably hit the earth first. (Pauses; then): And even if she did, what's in it for her? You gotta ask yourself that question. Bill? Marge? What the hell is in it for her anyway?

(Suddenly jumping to his feet):

I can't keep sittin'! And I don't feel good. Gas pains in my gut or something. I'm all full of stress.

(Pauses; then):

Ok, look, I'm gonna ask you something. If what God does is a

mystery, then how come when you put all the people
together who ever lived you can't solve it? (Pauses;
then): You got an answer for that? How come you can't
solve it? We can send people to the moon. Build cars. Television
sets. This camera that's staring at me like
nut. But if you put all our brains together like jellyfish in row on a
beach and wrap it around the world a few times you still couldn't
make a damn bit of sense out of what God does. How come? How
come your mother has to have a car accident on a sunny day on
her way to the goddamn laundromat and end up in a coma for
chrissakes when you can't even count the number of people she's
ever hurt 'cause there aren't any!?

(He stares severely; then):

That's no mystery. . . it's a crime. A real crime. What I'm gonna do
is a picnic compared to that. And if you're telling me that
somehow it's for her own good, you're crazier than a dog that's
got rabies. You'll never make any sense out of this'one, buddy.
And if you try, they might as well lock you up and throw away the
key.

(Starts pacing):

Jesus Christ! This world's the pits! The living pits! And she's just
one out of, Christ, I can't tell you how many people that are in the
same boat. And why? For what reason? Tell me!

(Pauses - staring, clearly baffled - anger rising):

And . . . why the hell . . . why the hell are all those people who
never did anythinq to anybody qetting shot in the ass all over
South America? Or over there in the mid-east? Even Ireland, for
chrissakes - which used to be run by the monks! Remember? And

Kosovo. You get this stuff on the news every night of the week!

(Pacing):

So why the hell does God let some piss-ant whacko dictator live for when he's got beautiful and decent people like Betty who goes to church her whole damn life and prays to Him and puts money in the plate and drinks His blood . . . and how does she end up? . . . how does she spell relief? suffering as much as the people she prayed to Him to help out?

And I'm telling you the list is beyond belief! You oughta see the ward she's on. They need computers just to keep track of them. All over the city. All over the city there's these dead people kept alive. In our own country, for chrissakes! America! Hey! Big dream! Big melting pot! From shore to shining shore. Hell, you put all the Betty's together and you'd get one HELL OF A BIG DREAM!! About no more SUFFERING! JESUS CHRIST! TAKE ME AWAY! I can't understand it. I just can't. All I can do is BEAT MY HEAD AGAINST THE WALL!

I can't look at anybody anymore without seeing them as a victim . . . yeah .. . as a victim of . . . something.

Aagh! Forget it. Just forget it. Try to think positive.

(Looks away, frowning. Then back):

Yeah, "positive." Look . . . if I had more time, I'd get out there and do something to help. You better believe it. I've had it up to here with people that just sit around whining . . . crying like babies about their problems and not doing anything about it. And I'm not talking politics, either. Politics is broken promises as far as I'm concerned. There's some that aren't bad. And all you can do is hope they stay clean. But what I'm talking about is "assistance." Getting involved inna organization--that isn't full of weirdos --to help people who are caving under. Not just poor people, either. I don't give a damn if you're rich or poor -- I've never met a poor person who was better than a rich person just because he is poor. If you're caving under you're caving under. I could pick from alot of organizations to get involved. Take your Red Cross, for example. Or March of Dimes. Or maybe something smaller . . . something in the neighborhood . . . like the Boy Scouts. Yeah. I'll bet I could help'em grow up to be good citizens . . . round off some of the rough edges in the world . . . reduce the crime rate.

(Pauses; then):

I'll   give you a statistic for you: Most of the crimes committed in America are committed by people who are caving under. Did you know that?

(He stares severely; then):

'Cause you need help.

(He nods; then):

Ok, I wanna bring this to a close, and let you go. As far as my last will and testament goes, it's in my safety deposit box over at Somona Savings bank. I won't go into it here, but it's not much. And as far as the law goes, I'm not sure what's gonna happen to my insurance policy . . . on account of beneficiaries not collecting from suicides. But you're both set pretty well anyhow. So. . . so much for that. What else is there to say except I'll tell you one more time that I love you both more than anything in the world. And keep your chin up no matter what. And forget what anybody's gonna say about me because it's probably not gonna be

nice. It's not even gonna be the truth. But it's gonna be for real . . .
'cause now I have the guts to stand up for what I believe, and
follow through on this. Your dad's a strong man.

Ok . . . so I just want you to know one more thing. Two more
things. The first is this: Betty's accident. I didn't tell you this
before. When you were right here afterwards. But . . . it was
meant for me. Or else, I mean, it might not have happened. And
that is . . . because . . . Betty had asked me to take the clothes
down to the laundromat. She was not feeling good. I said no.

(Pauses; then):

I don't like to hang around there. The only guys there are bums.
Or guys like me . . . without work. I see them, they see me. You
know what I mean? I just don't like to hang around there. So she
went, and not feeling good. She wasn't mad at me. She knows I
don't like that place. She only asked me because she was . . . sick.

(Stares; then):

Then I get the phone call. (Pauses) So, you see, it didn't have to
happen did it. But it did. And the only thing I can do is close shop.

(He drinks water, his hand shaking; then):

The second thing is this: this is not the first time I have done this .
. . gone out, I mean, and rented this camera to explain what I am
going to do. This is my third time. The first time, it was too
complicated. I could not get it to work right. The second time,
which was the last time . . . I do not think I said things right. I left
some of it out, too. But now I think I said things right, and it is all
there. I am feeling a little cold about it but it is all there just the
same. And who knows? Maybe feeling cold about it makes it
easier. Each time I seem to feel colder.

I just hope to God. . . that when I see Betty today . . I'm cold like ice. That I don't melt. I'm all frozen stiff inside sub-zero. . . or else . . . God help me. . . that if I should sit down beside her, rub her cheek, brush her hair back, I could . . . I could <u>thaw</u> . . . just enough. . .just enough to decide to give it one more day.

(He stares at the camera a moment, then stops it.
He crosses to EXIT as):

LIGHTS fade to Blackout

THE END